THE BIG BOOK OF
ACTIVITIES

C™

Peg Connery-Boyd

Illustrations by Scott Waddell

Published by Sourcebooks Jabberwocky, an imprint of Sourcebooks, Inc.
P.O. Box 4410, Naperville, Illinois 60567-4410
(630) 961-3900
Fax: (630) 961-2168
www.sourcebooks.com

Source of production: Versa Press, East Peoria, Illinois, USA
Date of production: February 2016
Run number: 5005855

Printed and bound in the United States of America.
VP 10 9 8 7 6 5 4 3 2 1

SLIDER™

RETIRED HEROES

Unscramble the names of the *Indians* heroes on the jerseys below.

AVERILL

_____

_____

_____

_____

_____

Solution is on page 49.

FOLLOW THE BALL
Which pitcher threw the strike?

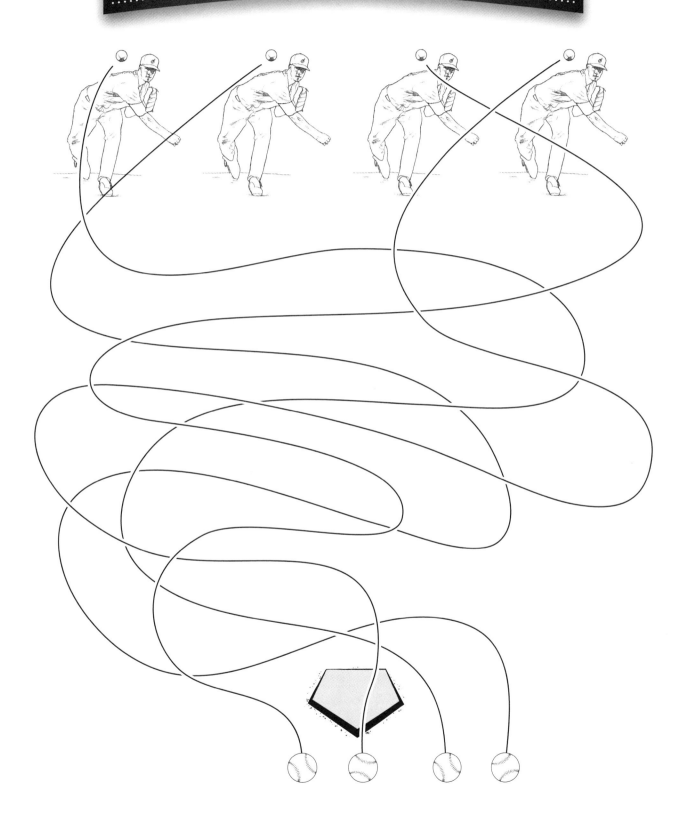

Solution is on page 49.

CONNECT THE DOTS

HINT!
A true *Indians* fan never leaves home without it!

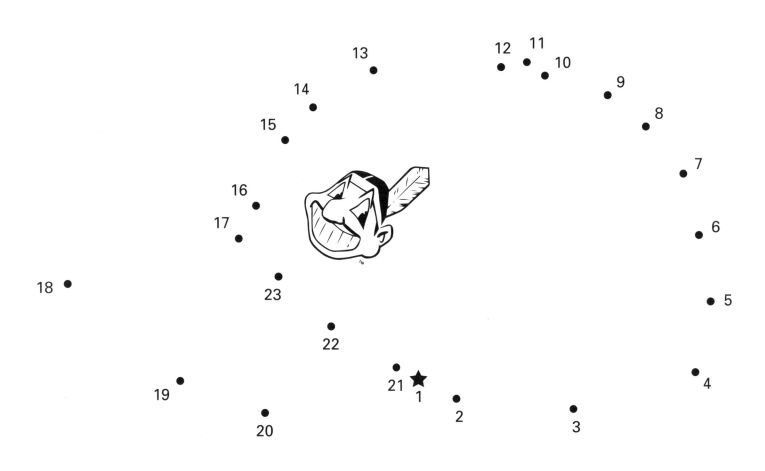

13

14

12   11

15   10

9

8

16

7

17

6

18

5

23

22

4

21   ★
1

19

2

20

3

4

FIND THE DIFFERENCES

Can you find all **three** differences between the two images below?

6

Solution is on page 50.

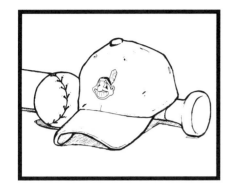 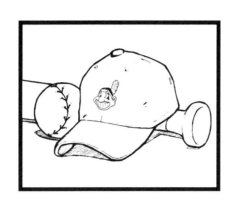 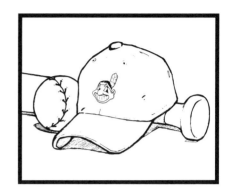

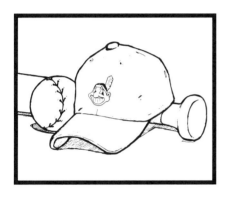 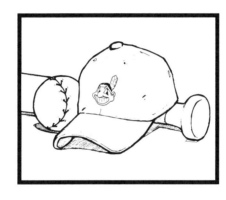 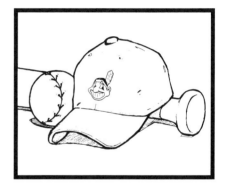

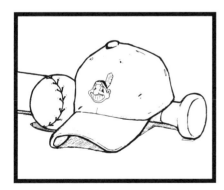 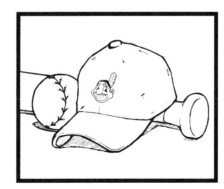 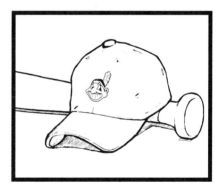

LET'S DRAW!
Use the grid to draw the *Indians* logo.

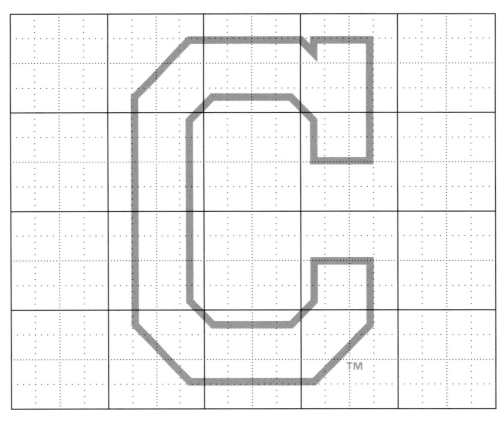

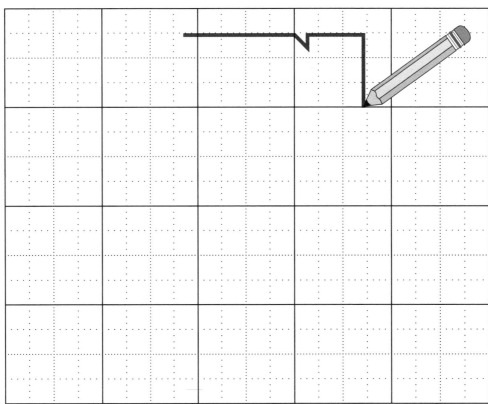

Use the key to decode the message.

KEY

= B	**C** = H	= O	= T
= E	= I	= R	= W
= N	= S		

Solution is on page 51.

LABEL THE PARTS OF A BASEBALL FIELD

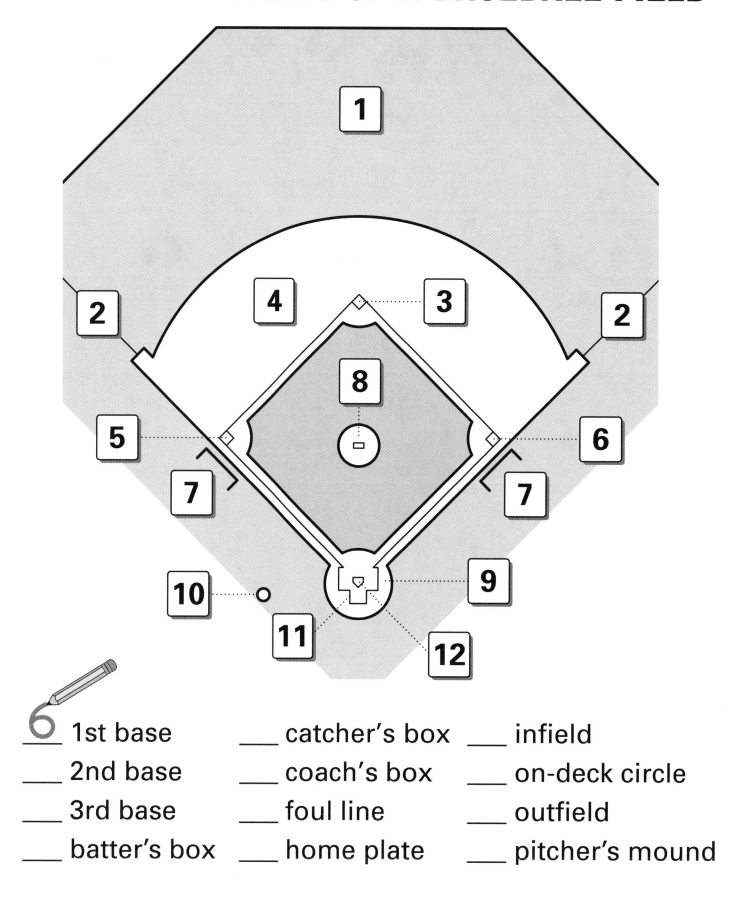

___ 1st base   ___ catcher's box   ___ infield

___ 2nd base   ___ coach's box   ___ on-deck circle

___ 3rd base   ___ foul line   ___ outfield

___ batter's box   ___ home plate   ___ pitcher's mound

    Solution is on page 52.

SCRAMBLE

Unscramble the letters of these *Progressive Field*™ snacks.

DOAS

_ _ _ _

OTH GDO

_ _ _   _ _ _

ROCPOPN

_ _ _ _ _ _ _

CIE MCEAR

_ _ _   _ _ _ _ _

ZEPRTEL

_ _ _ _ _ _ _

NUPTEAS

_ _ _ _ _ _ _

Solution is on page 52.

CONNECT THE DOTS

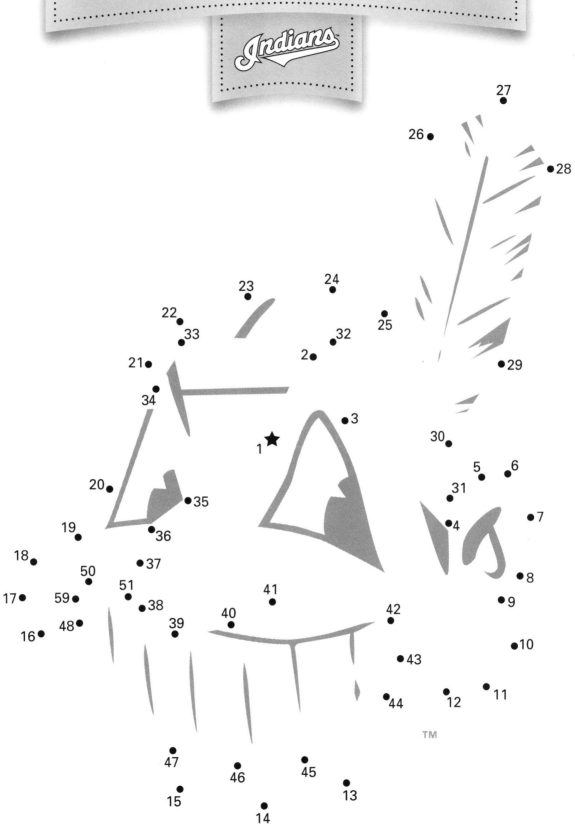

SLIDER IS SAFE!

```
C O C T L C T P Y C B
H A S I H L N R P L J
I H L K B E Y O I U Z
E N I C C V R G D B G
F G D O U E T R G H E
W Z E I Y L K E C O V
A J R N A A E S L U L
H F R K H N Y S Y S B
O G O O O D S I U E Q
O G P X G W H V Y J I
T H E J A K E E I D P
```

CHIEF WAHOO	CUYAHOGA	SLIDER
CLEVELAND	INDIANS	THE JAKE
CLUBHOUSE	PROGRESSIVE	TRIBE

Solution is on page 53.

BATTER UP!

CROSSWORD PUZZLE
Use your knowledge of baseball
to solve the puzzle.

Across

1. The pitcher stands on the pitcher's _____ when he throws the baseball.

5. After the batter hits the ball, he runs toward _____ base.

6. The player who throws the ball toward home plate for the batter to hit is called the _____.

9. To score a run, the player must touch _____ plate.

Down

2. The _____ calls the balls and strikes.

3. Each baseball player wears a baseball _____ on his head.

4. Three strikes and you're _____!

7. The player who crouches behind home plate is called the _____.

8. A baseball player wears a _____ on his hand to catch the ball.

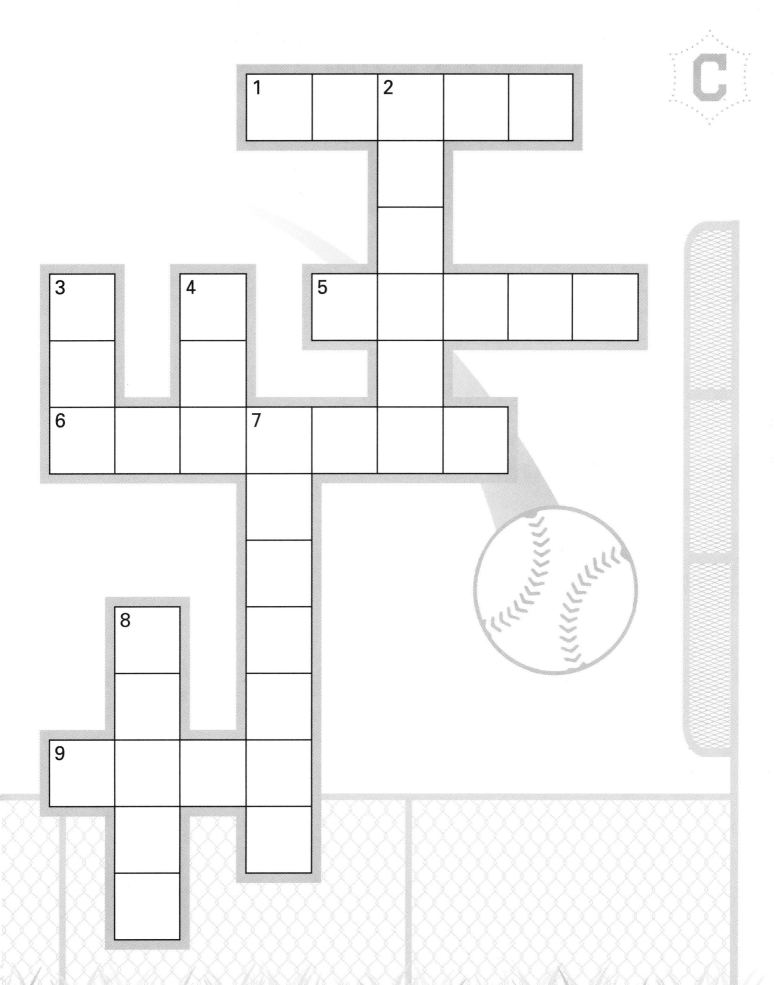

Solution is on page 53.

CONNECT THE DOTS

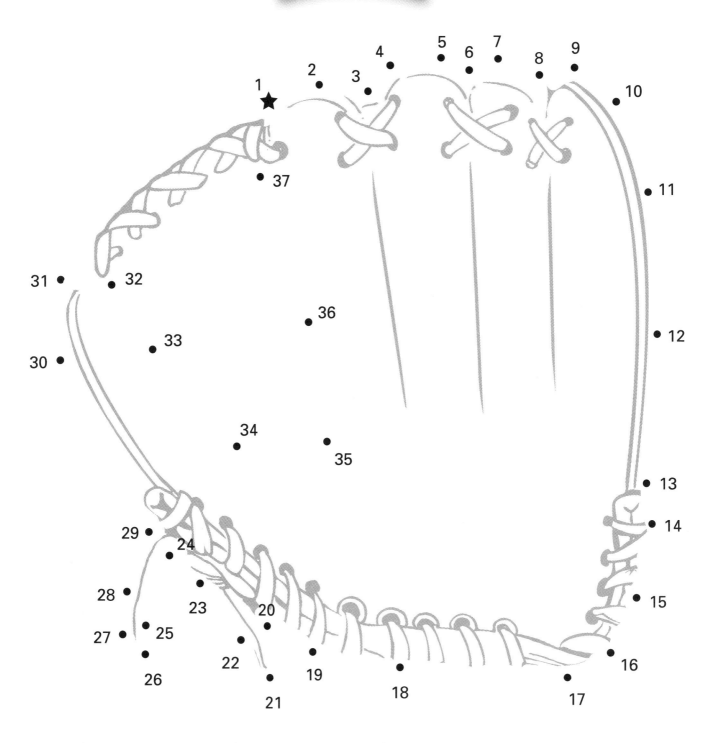

I HAD A GREAT DAY AT PROGRESSIVE FIELD

by _____
(your name)

It was a _____ day in _____.
(weather word)   (month)

The *Indians* were playing the _____ at
(team name)

Progressive Field. We took a _____ to get
(car / train / bus)

to Cleveland. I snacked on some _____
(food)

and _____ while we watched the game.
(food)

I was so excited to see _____
(player name)

play today. He's my favorite player! The *Indians*

_____ the game. The score was ____ to ____.
(won / lost)   (score)   (score)

Baseball is my favorite sport, but I also like to

watch _____. I can't wait to come back to
(sport)

Progressive Field!

A HOME RUN FOR THE *Indians*!

SCRAMBLE

Unscramble the letters of these baseball words.

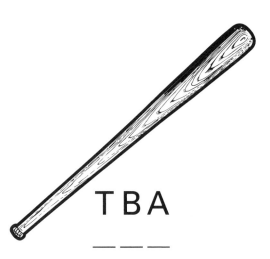

TBA

_ _ _

APC

_ _ _

PMRIEU

_ _ _ _ _ _

SYERJE

_ _ _ _ _ _

VOEGL

_ _ _ _ _

EBAS

_ _ _ _

FOLLOW THE BALL

The outfielder is about to make a catch!
Which batter will be out?

Solution is on page 54.

S _ _ _ _ _ _ _

_ _ _ _ _ _

_ _ _ _ _ _ _

KEY

= C	= H	= R	= V
= E	= I	= S	
= G	= N	= T	

Solution is on page 55.

WORD SEARCH

```
T T P L A Y O F F S D
E W U T H I D E N N N
O S E P F G C O S A B
B E O N W Y I R C S A
F R L U A P A I J G L
T I M D M T R U Q B L
H E V A S E I Y W F P
D S H L M F B O L X A
Y C L A A R Z U N W R
C A F L E Y X Q Q A K
V S S D E R O Z O U L
```

ALL STARS	CHAMPIONS	PLAYOFFS
AMERICAN	DERBY	SERIES
BALLPARK	NATIONAL	TROPHY

HIDDEN PICTURE

Use the key to color the shapes below and reveal the hidden picture.

KEY

A = Brown   **B = Blue**   **C = Purple**   **D = Green**   **E = Yellow**   **F = Black**

HINT!
Color inside the lines!

Use the key to decode the message.

T __ __ __ __

__ __ __ __ __ __ __

'

__ __ __ __ __ __ __ __

!

__ __ __

KEY

= A	= H	= N	= S	= Y
= D	= I	= O	= T	
= E	= K	= R	= U	

Solution is on page 56.

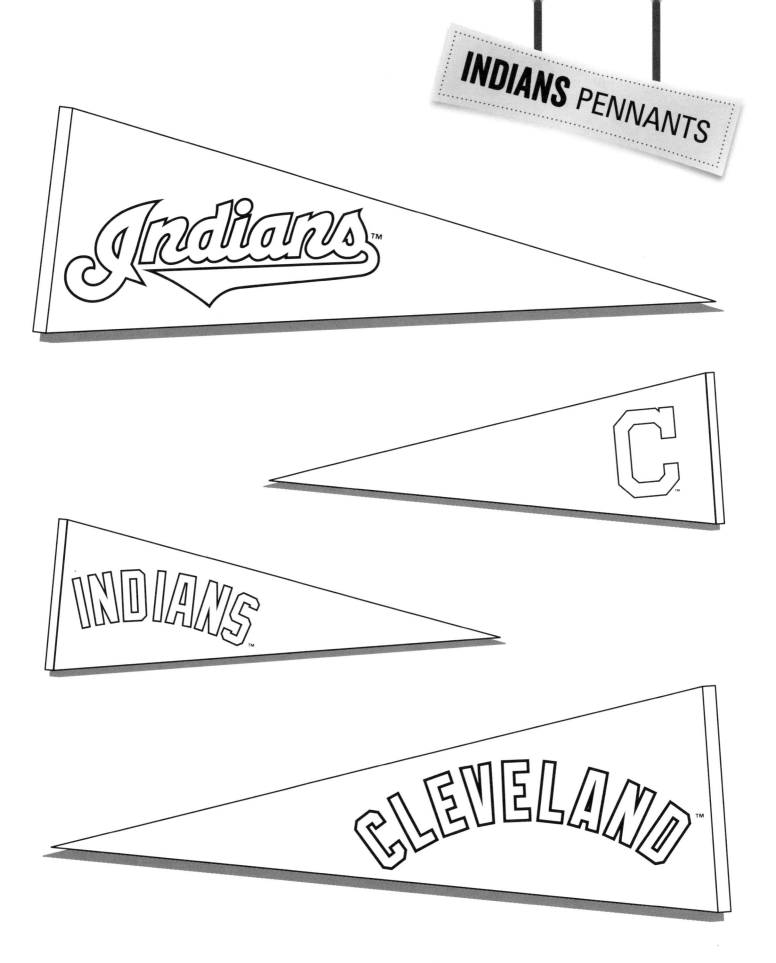

WHAT'S IN A NAME?

How many words can you make using letters found in the two words below?

CLEVELAND INDIANS

Example: SEAL   VINE

1 _____   11 _____

2 _____   12 _____

3 _____   13 _____

4 _____   14 _____

5 _____   15 _____

6 _____   16 _____

7 _____   17 _____

8 _____   18 _____

9 _____   19 _____

10 _____   20 _____

Solution is on page 56.

MY BASEBALL CARD

SIDE 1:
Draw yourself!

_____
(your name)

#
_____
(number)

Indians™

SIDE 2:
Complete your stats!

Indians™

Age: _____

Position: _____

Height: _____

Weight: _____

Circle one!

I bat (righty / lefty)
I throw (righty / lefty)

_____ has shown excellent
(your name)
sportsmanship this year!

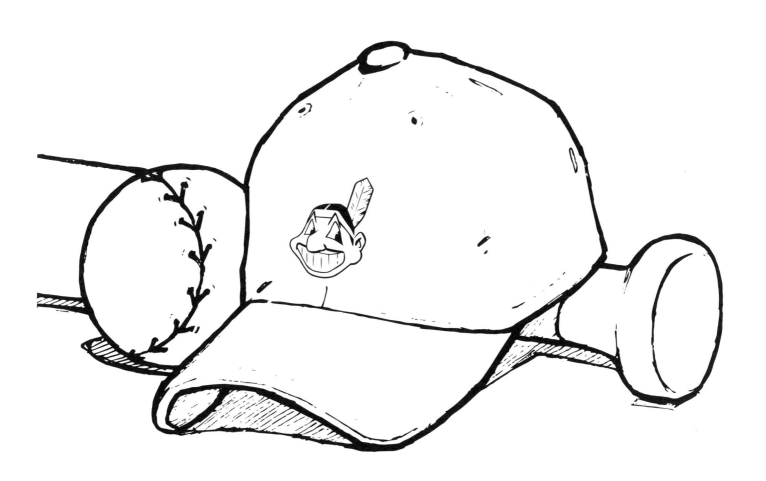

WHAT'S THE SCORE?

Add the runs to find out which team won the game.

Example:	1	2	3	4	5	6	7	8	9	R
TIGERS	0	1	0	0	2	0	0	0	0	3
INDIANS	0	0	1	0	0	1	0	0	2	4

Game 1:	1	2	3	4	5	6	7	8	9	R
TIGERS	0	0	0	0	1	0	2	0	0	
INDIANS	0	2	0	0	1	0	1	1	0	

Game 2:	1	2	3	4	5	6	7	8	9	R
TWINS	0	0	1	0	0	0	0	0	1	
INDIANS	0	3	0	0	2	0	0	2	0	

Game 3:	1	2	3	4	5	6	7	8	9	R
ROYALS	0	3	1	2	0	1	0	1	0	
INDIANS	0	1	0	1	2	0	1	0	1	

Game 4:	1	2	3	4	5	6	7	8	9	R
WHITE SOX	1	1	1	0	1	0	3	0	0	
INDIANS	0	4	1	0	1	1	0	0	2	

Solution is on page 57.

START HERE

LET'S DRAW!

Use the grid to draw the *MLB*™ logo.

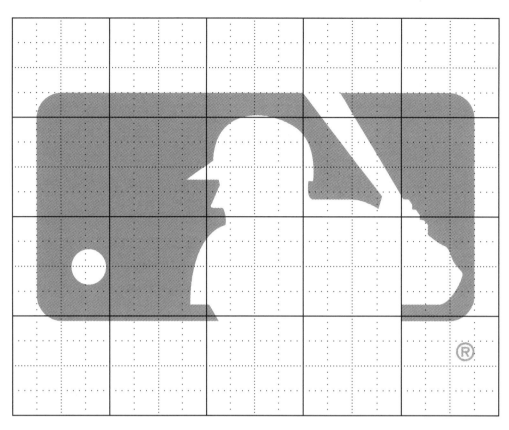

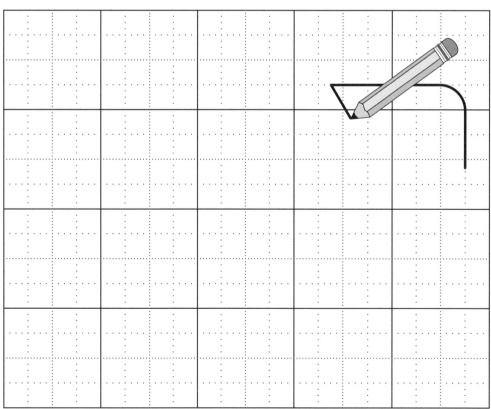

```
B H A R D E R G B E H
O J B D T Z D C E D T
L T L O M V A O O F T
L A M B U F V V Y J E
S G J Y C D E E G G M
L E M O N D R L F L M
Q Y N W I P I E L P T
Y B U O Z E L S A E M
H V B U G T L K R U R
B G C O L A V I T O Y
E H N T G K P A M D C
```

AVERILL	COVELESKI	HARDER
BOUDREAU	DOBY	LAJOIE
COLAVITO	FELLER	LEMON

ONE LUCKY Indians FAN

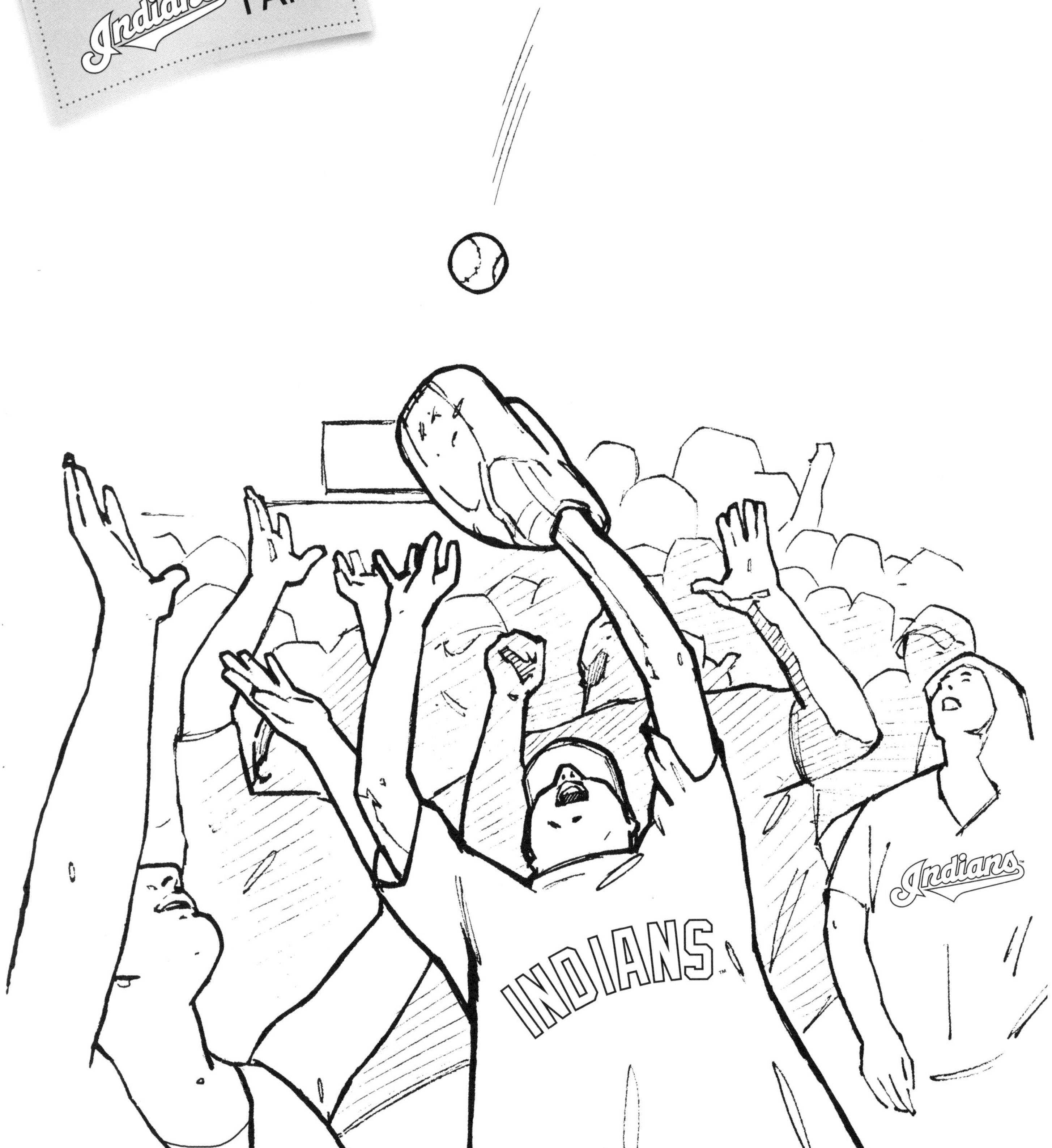

Use the key to decode the message.

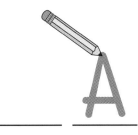

TAKE ME

OUT TO THE

BALLGAME

KEY

= A	= G	= L	= T
= B	= H	= M	= U
= E	= K	= O	

FIND THE DIFFERENCES

Can you find all **four** differences between the two images below?

Solution is on page 59.

SCRAMBLE

Unscramble the letters of these baseball positions.

ITCHREP

P I T C H E R

CAHTERC

_ _ _ _ _ _ _

RIFTS

_ _ _ _ _

SABMANE

_ _ _ _ _ _ _

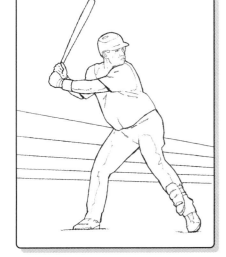

ERTTAB

_ _ _ _ _ _

TUOLIEFDRE

_ _ _ _ _ _ _ _ _ _

Solution is on page 59.

WHAT'S IN A NAME?

How many words can you make using letters found in the three words below?

MAJOR LEAGUE BASEBALL

Example: AREA   BEAR

1 _____

2 _____

3 _____

4 _____

5 _____

6 _____

7 _____

8 _____

9 _____

10 _____

11 _____

12 _____

13 _____

14 _____

15 _____

16 _____

17 _____

18 _____

19 _____

20 _____

          Solution is on page 60.

IS THE BATTER SAFE?

Follow the maze to find out!

OUT!

SAFE!

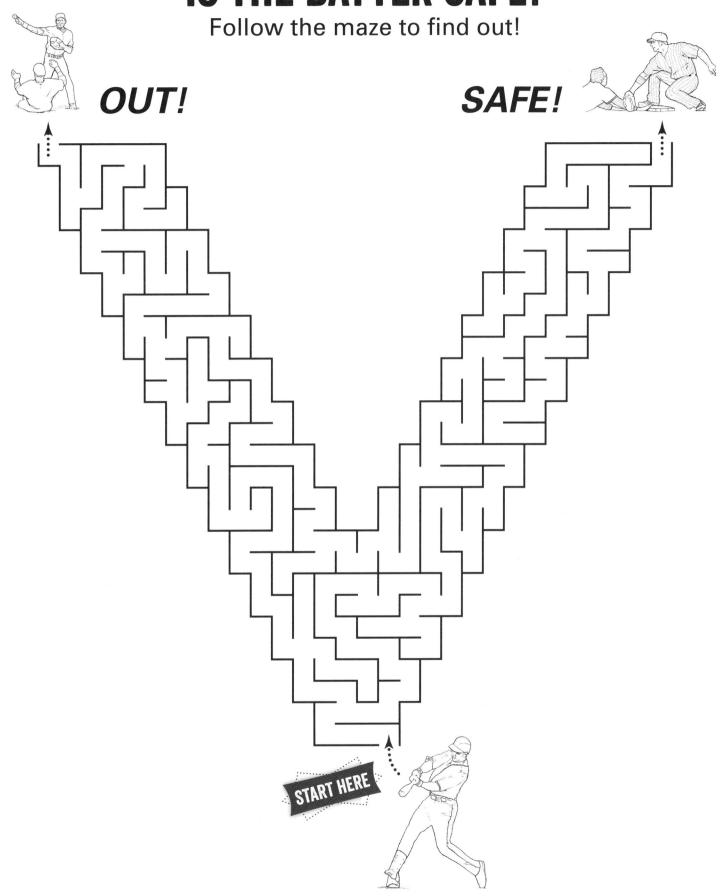

START HERE

Solution is on page 60.

CROSSWORD PUZZLE

Use your knowledge of the
Indians to solve the puzzle.

Across

2. In 1997, the *Indians* played in the *World Series* against the *Florida* _____.

4. Players wear the insignia of *Chief* _____ on the left sleeve of their uniforms.

7. *Indians* number 19 was retired in honor of Hall of Fame pitcher Bob _____.

8. Goodyear, _____, is home to the *Indians* Spring Training facility.

9. _____ is the name of the beloved *Indians* mascot.

Down

1. _____ *Field* is the name of the home ballpark of the *Cleveland Indians*.

3. In 1975, Frank _____ became the first African American manager in *Major League Baseball* when he was hired as player-manager for the *Indians*.

5. _____ Park at *Progressive Field* is home of the *Indians* Hall of Fame.

6. *Progressive Field* was formerly named _____ *Field* and is often referred to as "The Jake."

HIDDEN PICTURE

Use the key to color the shapes below and reveal the hidden picture.

KEY

A = Dark Blue   B = Light Blue   C = Light Gray   D = Dark Gray (or black)   E = Tan

HINT!
Color inside the lines!

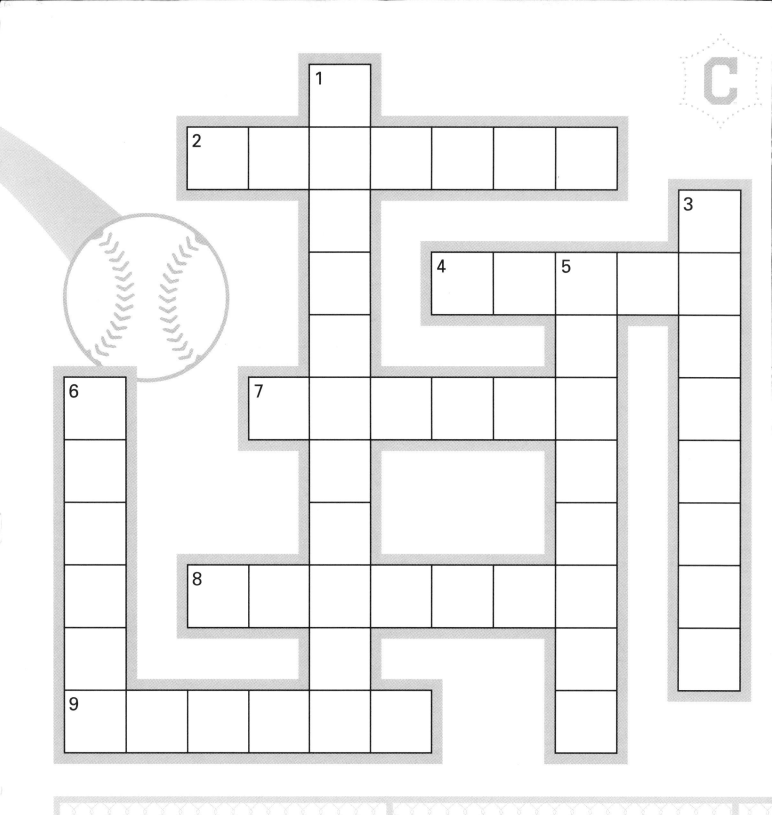

Solution is on page 61.

WORD SEARCH

```
C T J I Q U E K R R W
P A I U D L Z K T L V
E M T G P U H C U P B
N Z S C M B G O A T A
U P Y T H L F O K P S
C C D U R E Y B U I E
F V W U R I R S I T B
O W K I O V K E R C A
Q X P G L O V E Q H L
E M Z D R G Z X T E L
U Z S O G S M T N R Q
```

BASEBALL	DUGOUT	PITCHER
CAP	FOUL	STRIKE
CATCHER	GLOVE	UMPIRE

Solution is on page 61.

WHICH **SLIDER** MASCOT LOOKS DIFFERENT FROM THE REST?

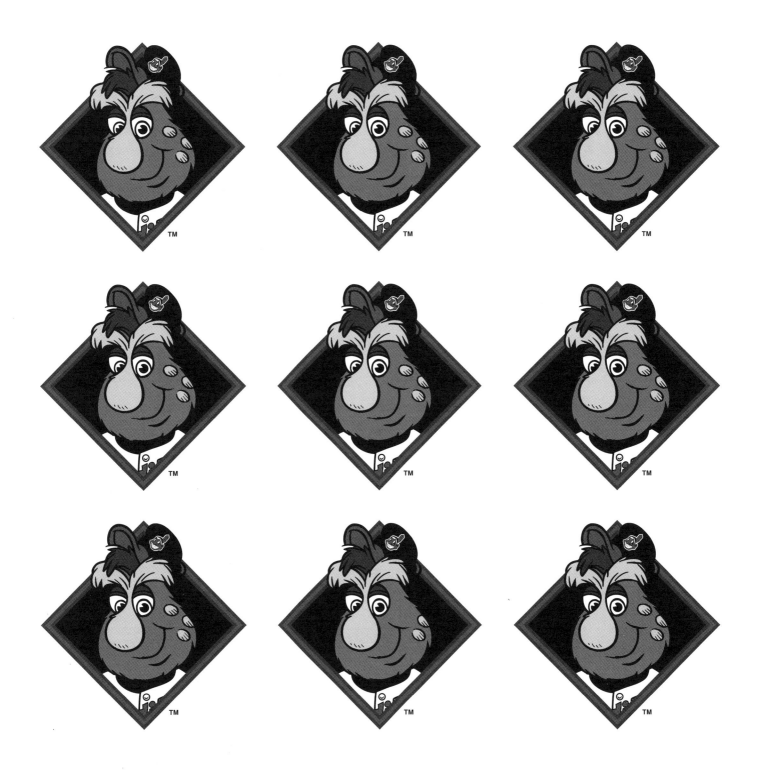

Solution is on page 62.

SOLUTIONS

Page 2

Page 3

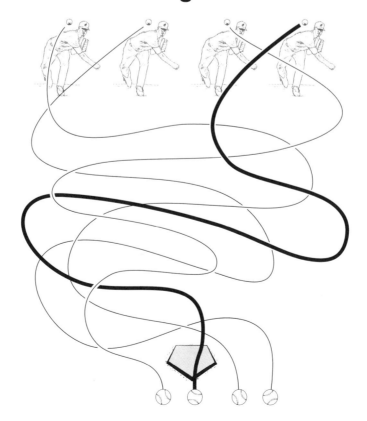

Page 5

Page 6

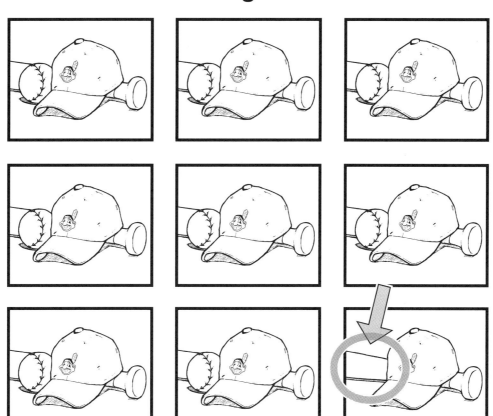

Page 9

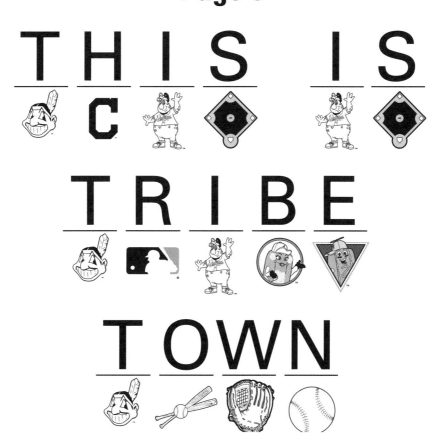

Page 10

6 1st base   **11** catcher's box   **4** infield

3 2nd base   **7** coach's box   **10** on-deck circle

5 3rd base   **2** foul line   **1** outfield

9 batter's box   **12** home plate   **8** pitcher's mound

Page 12

SODA

HOT DOG

POPCORN

ICE CREAM

PRETZEL

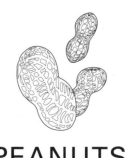

PEANUTS

Page 16

Page 19

Page 24

BAT

CAP

UMPIRE

JERSEY

GLOVE

BASE

Page 25

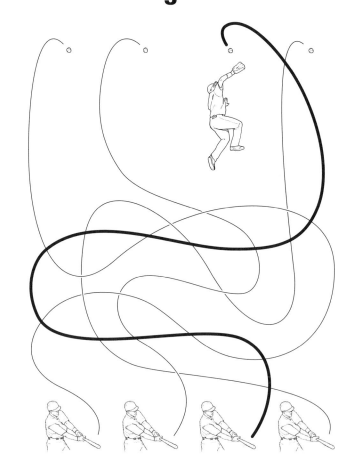

Page 26

SEVENTH

INNING

STRETCH

Page 27

55

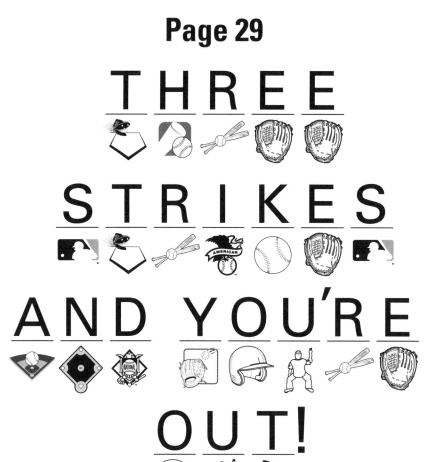

THREE
STRIKES
AND YOU'RE
OUT!

Page 31

Below are just a few examples of words that could be made with these letters.

<u>C L E V E L A N D</u>   <u>I N D I A N S</u>

ace	cell	die	island	lens	sad	sever
advice	clean	dine	ladies	level	said	side
aid	cleanse	disc	land	lilac	sail	sled
alien	dance	easel	lane	line	sand	slice
and	deal	end	lead	linen	scald	slid
call	deadlines	ice	lean	nail	scale	slide
calve	decline	ideal	lease	navel	scan	snail
candies	den	idle	leave	need	scene	veil
candle	dial	insane	lend	niece	send	vice

Page 34

Game 1:	1	2	3	4	5	6	7	8	9	R
TIGERS	0	0	0	0	1	0	2	0	0	3
INDIANS	0	2	0	0	1	0	1	1	0	5

Game 2:	1	2	3	4	5	6	7	8	9	R
TWINS	0	0	1	0	0	0	0	0	1	2
INDIANS	0	3	0	0	2	0	0	2	0	7

Game 3:	1	2	3	4	5	6	7	8	9	R
ROYALS	0	3	1	2	0	1	0	1	0	8
INDIANS	0	1	0	1	2	0	1	0	1	6

Game 4:	1	2	3	4	5	6	7	8	9	R
WHITE SOX	1	1	1	0	1	0	3	0	0	7
INDIANS	0	4	1	0	1	1	0	0	2	9

Page 35

Page 37

```
B (H A R D E R) G B E H
O J (B) D T Z D (C) E D T
(L T L O M V A O) O F T
L A M B U F V V Y J E
S G J Y C D E E G G M
(L E M O N) D R L F L M
Q Y N W I P I E L P T
Y B U O Z E L S A E M
H V B U G T L K R U R)
B G (C O L A V I T O) Y
E H N T G K P A M D C
```

Page 39

TAKE ME

OUT TO THE

BALLGAME

Page 40

Page 41

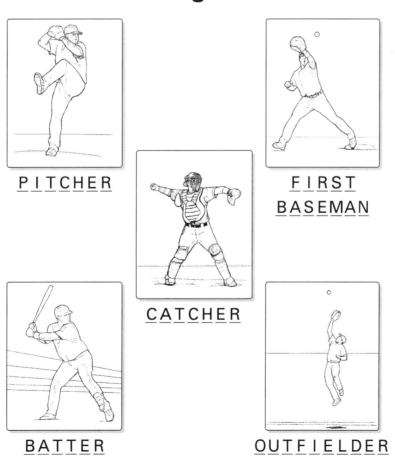

PITCHER

FIRST BASEMAN

CATCHER

BATTER

OUTFIELDER

Page 42

Below are just a few examples of words that could be made with these letters.

M A J O R L E A G U E B A S E B A L L

ajar	beam	bull	gore	meal	reel	seem
alas	bear	ease	lamb	mole	roll	sell
also	bell	else	lame	mule	rule	slab
area	blob	game	lobe	muse	saga	slam
aura	blue	gear	lube	ogre	sage	soar
ball	blur	germ	lure	oral	sale	some
barb	boar	glee	male	rage	seal	sour
bare	bomb	glue	mall	real	seam	urge
base	bulb	goal	mars	ream	sear	user

Page 43

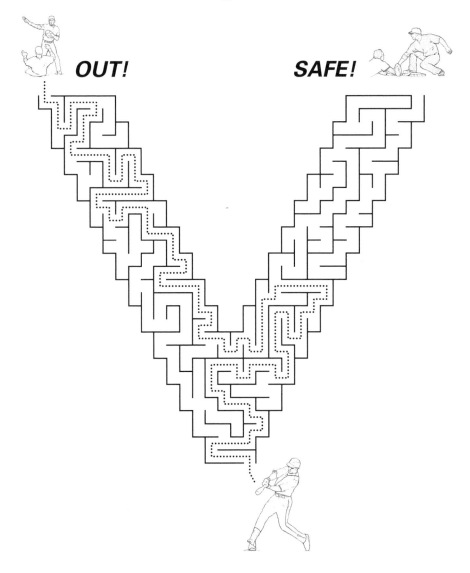

OUT!   SAFE!

Page 45

Page 47

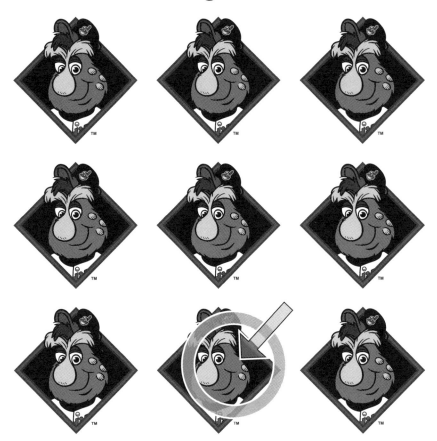